Debbie Humphreys

DOGS IN JUMPERS

12 practical knitting projects

T0340519

COLLINS & BROWN

This book is dedicated to Bruno, my first and much loved whippet, whose shivering inspired my renewed love of knitting, without which this book would never have been created.

Printed in 2019 by Pavilion
An imprint of HarperCollins*Publishers*
1 London Bridge Street
London SE1 9GF

www.harpercollins.co.uk

HarperCollins*Publishers*
Macken House
39/40 Mayor Street Upper
Dublin 1
D01 C9W8
Ireland

Copyright © Pavilion Books Company Ltd
2015, 2019

Text and pattern copyright © Debbie Humphreys
2015, 2019

All rights reserved. No part of this publication may be reproduced, stored in a retrieval system or transmitted in any form or by any means, electronic, mechanical, photocopying, recording or otherwise, without the prior written permission of the copyright owner. The patterns contained in this book and the items created from them are for personal use only. Commercial use of either the patterns or items made from them is strictly prohibited.

ISBN 978-1-911624-99-8

A CIP catalogue record for this book is available from the British Library.

10 9 8 7 6 5 4 3 2

Reproduction by Mission Productions Ltd, Hong Kong
Printed by Oriental Press, UAE

www.pavilionbooks.com

Photography by Kerry Jordan of
  Whippet Snippets, except portrait of
  Bruno on page 7 by Maryanne Hawes
Illustrations by Kate Haxell

All our photographs were taken on location at the delightful Bredgar and Wormshill Light Railway during the winter months when no trains were running.

FSC
www.fsc.org

MIX
Paper | Supporting
responsible forestry
FSC™ C007454

Acknowledgements

Writing this book has long been a dream for me and several people helped make it happen.

A special thanks goes out to:
My yarn suppliers, knitters and pattern checkers.
My technical support – Kate Haxell and Marilyn Wilson.
My photographer, Kerry Jordan, a most patient and talented lady.
My Uncle Bill and Auntie Irene for the use of their stunning grounds for the photos.
My dog models, those still here and those no longer.
Everyone at Pavilion for believing I could do it!

A special huge thank you to my wonderful husband, David, always by my side, always supporting me and for taking on all domestic duties while I knitted my way through a long winter to bring you this lovely book. Without him I fear we might have starved!

An enormous thank you must go out to my Knitting for Redhound ladies who have diligently knitted and checked every line of every pattern and who continue to knit gorgeous garments for my charity auctions allowing us to raise funds for many dog charities.

Finally, to Izzy Holton for all her hard work and patience in the production of this paperback edition.

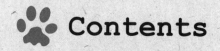 # Contents

Introduction

I haven't always been a knitter. I was taught to knit by my mum in the early 1970's but I soon lost interest, who wanted to knit a jumper when you could pop down to Chelsea Girl and buy the latest Skinny Rib?

It was many years later when I welcomed a shivering whippet into my life that I was inspired to pick the needles up and attempt to make him a jumper. Bruno was most patient with my first creations, there were dropped stitches, odd shapes and many that didn't fit, but I discovered that I loved having a go, making something for my dog with love, an item to keep him warm and happy.

Knitting soon became my obsession – I joined every course available, developing my skills, learning new techniques and stretching my abilities. Bruno became the object of much envy with his hound friends, leading me to set up my business Redhound for Dogs – creating clothing to keep whippets warm, dry and happy.

I dreamt that one day I would write a book of stylish patterns so that other dog loving knitters could create a warm jumper for their constant companions. Dogs in Jumpers is the result of that dream.

Bruno is sadly no longer at my side, but my love of knitting has led to many dogs benefiting from the clicking of needles to create jumpers from the patterns he inspired. I now host an annual auction of jumpers raising much needed funds for dog charities – over £5000 at the time of writing. With the help of an army of wonderful knitters we hope to continue to raise much more through our joint love of knitting and dogs.

My goal is to marry style with function and so you won't find a jumper in this book to fit a furry sheep dog. The dogs in this book are those that feel the cold – mostly of the sighthound family – the breed I love and share my life with.

Dogs come in many shapes and sizes. The measurements for each pattern will help you see

if the finished jumper will fit your dog. If you think all but the length will be good, knit the top panel a little longer, but don't forget to do the same on the underneath. Don't be afraid to lay your knitting on your dog to see how it's progressing. The most important thing to remember is that your dog won't complain if it isn't perfect!

I now share my life with whippets George and Winnie who take pleasure from chewing needles and unravelling wool! So, if you have a young one around my advice is to keep your knitting safely packed away and out of reach!

Debbie Humphreys

PAW-ABILITY LEVEL

Each project has been paw-rated – one paw being easy, ideal for beginners – up to 3 paws for more challenging knits.

YARN CHOICES

Buster, Bruno, Daisy and Frankie's jumpers call for Aran weight but all the other projects have successfully been knitted in DK yarn. If you are changing yarn, do a tension square and compare to the pattern. This will avoid mistakes in the sizing department!

🐾 FACT FILE

BUSTER
....

Breed: Greyhound.
Character: A very loving, happy boy, especially during family get-togethers as these provide plenty of counter-surfing opportunities!
Happiest When: Walking on Camber Sands.
Will Do Anything For: Treats – any kind!
Naughtiest Habit: Raiding the waste bin.
Favourite Treat: Fresh trout.
Hobbies Include: Sleeping on the sofa with his teddy bear.

Buster's Cosy Chunky Cable Jumper

I designed this jumper knowing that the green and the chunky cable would look fantastic on Buster. Mark off the pattern rows as you complete them. Knitting in the round makes the cable easier as you are looking at the right side of the work, so the pattern is a pleasure to knit.

Size
Dog measurements
Neck 43cm
Shoulder 33cm
Chest 71–75cm
Length 70–75cm
See Measure Your Dog (page 79)

Garment measurements
Neck 40cm unstretched
Chest 61cm unstretched
Length 58cm plus collar

Yarn
8 x 50g balls of Rowan Felted Tweed Aran in Glade 733 or any Aran weight yarn (check tension)

Needles and equipment
One each of 40cm 4.5mm and 80cm 5mm circular needle
Set of 4 x 4mm double-pointed needles
Cable needle
4 stitch markers
3 stitch holders
Knitter's sewing needle

Tension
27sts and 26 rows over central cable patt to a 10cm square using 5mm needles.

Abbreviations
See page 78.

Notes
This jumper is knitted for the most part in the round on a circular needle, and the pattern assumes that the rs is the inside of the knitting.

JUMPER
Starting at the neck edge and with 4.5mm circular needle, cast on 105sts. Ensuring that the work is not twisted, place marker and join the round.
Round 1: [k3, p2] to end.
This round sets rib patt. Cont in patt until rib measures 23cm from cast on edge.
The inside of the tube of knitting is k3, p2 rib and will be the rs of the neck rib when the neck is rolled down, so now turn the work inside out and work the neck inc.
Next round (inc round): [k3, p1, M1, p1] to end. *(126sts)*
Next round: [k3, p3] to end.

Cont in patt until rib measures 26cm from cast on edge. Change to 5mm circular needle. Divide sts to form back sts, first leg sts, chest sts and second leg sts as folls:

Round 1: k6, p3, [k9, p3] 5 times, k6 (*75sts for back*), place marker, [p3, k3] twice, p3 (*15sts for first leg*), place marker, [k3, p3] 3 times, k3 (*21sts for chest*), place marker, [p3, k3] twice, p3 (*15sts for second leg*).

Round 2 (inc round): k1, M1, k5, p3, [k9, p3] 5 times, k5, M1, k1 across back sts (*77sts for back*), slm, rib as set across leg and chest sts, slm.

Round 3 (cable round): k7, p3, [k3, C6F, p3] 5 times, k7 across back sts, slm, rib as set across leg and chest sts, slm.

Round 4: k7, p3, [k9, p3] 5 times, k7 across back sts, slm, rib as set across leg and chest sts, slm.

Round 5: k7, p3, [k9, p3] 5 times, k7 across back sts, slm, rib as set across leg and chest sts, slm.

Round 6 (inc round): k1, M1, k6, p3, [k9, p3] 5 times, k6, M1, k1 across back sts (*79sts for back*), slm, rib as set across leg and chest sts, slm.

Round 7 (cable round): k8, p3, [C6B, k3, p3] 5 times, k8 across back sts, slm, rib as set across leg and chest sts, slm.

Round 8: k8, p3, [k9, p3] 5 times, k8 across back sts, slm, rib as set across leg and chest sts, slm.

These 8 rounds set patt. Cont in patt, inc on every round 2 and 6 until there are 89 back sts on and 140sts in total. (*89sts for back, 15sts for first leg, 21sts for chest, 15sts for second leg*)

Cont without shaping until work measures 35cm from cast on edge. At this stage you can adjust length to suit your dog.

Make leg holes

Next round: work back sts in patt, rib across 15 first leg sts then put them onto a stitch holder, rib across 21 chest sts, rib across 15 second leg sts then

put them onto a stitch holder.
Next round: work back sts in patt, cast on 15sts for first leg, rib across 21 chest sts, cast on 15sts for second leg, ensuring the markers are in place again. Cont in the round in patt as set until work measures 20cm from leg holes.

Shape under chest

Next round (dec round): work back sts in patt, rib across first leg sts to 2sts before marker, k2tog (*14sts for first leg*), slm, rib across 21 chest sts, slm,

BACK   **FRONT**

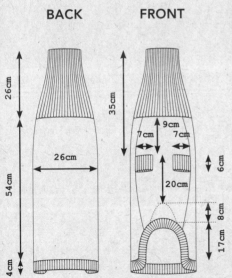

k2tog, rib across rem leg sts *(14sts for second leg)*.

Cont to dec as set, altering the dec worked (either k2tog or p2tog) to suit patt, until all 15sts of each leg are eliminated. On the last dec round, remove the markers.

Cont without decreasing until work measures 38cm from leg holes, finishing with patt round 7.

Next round: work back sts in patt as set for round 8, rib across 21 chest sts then put them onto a stitch holder.

Work back sts, working back and forth on the circular needle.

Row 1 (rs): k13, p3, [k9, p3] 5 times, k13.

Row 2: p13, k3, [p9, k3] 5 times, p13.

Row 3 (cable row): k13, p3, [k3, C6F, p3] 5 times, k13.

Row 4: p13, k3, [p9, k3] 5 times, p13.

Row 5: k13, p3, [k9, p3] 5 times, k13.

Row 6: p13, k3, [p9, k3] 5 times, p13.

Row 7 (cable row): k13, p3, [C6B, k3, p3] 5 times, k13.

Row 8: p13, k3, [p9, k3] 5 times, p13.

These 8 rows set cable patt with st st borders.

Shape rump

Dec on every row 1 and row 5 of cable patt rep by working k2tog, 3sts in from each edge, then working rem sts of st st border until 71sts remain and work measures 54cm from bottom of neck rib along centre back of jumper.

Rib border

With 4.5mm circular needle, k2, k2tog, [p3, k3] 10 times, p3, k2tog, k2, pick up 27sts along the right side back panel edge, [k3, p3] 3 times, k3 across chest sts on stitch holder, pick up 27sts along the left side back panel edge to complete the round.

Place marker and commence working in the round.

Next round: [k3, p3] to end.

Rep this round until rib measures 4cm, then cast off loosely in patt. It is important that you don't cast off too tightly, as this edge needs to stretch over the dog's chest when pulling the jumper on and off.

LEG HOLE BORDER

Working with the jumper rs out and using 4mm dpns, on one leg hole pick up 21sts across cast off leg hole sts, then rib the 15sts from the holder. Divide the sts between 4 dpns (9sts on each needle).

Round 1: k3, place marker, [p3, k3] to end.

Work in rib as set for 14 rounds. Cast off loosely in patt.

Work second leg hole border to match.

TO MAKE UP

Weave in all loose ends.

Tip: Try on your dog as you knit to check the fit after you have done all the shoulder increases – you might need to work a few extra rows.

🐾 FACT FILE

MISS
DAISY DUKE

Breed: Miniature Smooth-Haired Dachshund.

Character: Daisy has a big character! She knows what she wants and she knows how to get it!

Happiest When: Her tummy is full, settled on her human dad's knee.

Will Do Anything For: Food.

Naughtiest Habit: Pulling her brother's tail telling him it's playtime.

Favourite Treat: Sprats.

Hobbies Include: Barking, running, eating, sleeping and chasing pheasants.

Daisy's Really Rather Good Jumper

I wanted textured stripes to flatter a dachshund's long body and this easy twist stitch is great in what is effectively a rib pattern. There is shaping to accommodate the deep chest of these little dogs and short legs so that the jumper does not slip off when your dog runs around.

Size
Dog measurements
Neck 24–30cm
Shoulder 12–14cm
Chest 38–44cm
Length 35–39cm
See Measure Your Dog
  (page 79)

Garment measurements
Neck 26cm unstretched
Chest 40cm unstretched
Length 35cm plus collar

Yarn
3 x 50g balls of Rowan Felted
  Tweed Aran in Dark Violet 738.

Also works in DK yarn but
might come up a little smaller

Needles and equipment
Pair each of 4mm and 4.5mm
  knitting needles
4 safety pins to use as markers
  for leg holes
Knitter's sewing needle

Tension
22sts and 24 rows over twist rib
  patt to a 10cm square using
  4.5mm needles.

Abbreviations
See page 78.

TOP PANEL
Starting at the lower edge and
with 4mm needles, cast on 50sts.
Set rib patt
Row 1 (rs): k4, [p2, k2] to last
6sts, p2, k4.
Row 2: k2, [p2, k2] to end.
Rep last 2 rows 4 times more.
Row 11 (dec row): k2, k2tog,
[p2, k2] to last 6sts, p2, k4.
(49sts)
Row 12: knit the knit sts and
purl the purl sts.
Change to 4.5mm needles.
Set twist rib patt
Row 1 (rs): p1, [Tw2, p3] to last
3sts, Tw2, p1.
Row 2: k1, [p2, k3] to last 3sts,
p2, k1.
These 2 rows set twist rib patt.
Cont in patt until work measures
23cm from cast on edge, ending
with a ws row.
Shape leg
Next row (rs): cast off 4sts, patt
to end. *(45sts)*

Next row: cast off 4sts, patt to end. *(41sts)*
Cont in rib patt as set until work measures 7cm from start of leg shaping.
Place a marker at each edge of work to mark end of leg hole.
Cont in rib patt as set until work measures 12cm from start of leg shaping, dec 1st in centre of last row.
With rs facing put these 40sts onto a stitch holder and set aside.

UNDER PANEL

Starting at the lower edge and with 4.5mm needles, cast on 18sts.
Set rib patt
Row 1 (rs): k3, [p2, k3] twice, p2, k3.
Row 2: k1, p2, [k2, p3] twice, k2, p2, k1.
Rep last 2 rows twice more.
Row 7 (inc row): k2, M1, k1, [p2, k3] twice, p2, k1, M1, k2. *(20sts)*
Row 8: k1, p3, [k2, p3] twice, k2, p3, k1.
Keeping edge sts as st st, cont to inc and work into st st on every 4th row as set until there are 38sts. Knit the first and

last stitch on ws rows to give a neat edge.
Cont without shaping until work measures 18cm from cast on edge, ending with a ws row.
Shape leg
Next row (rs): cast off 4sts, k8, [p2, k3] twice, p2, k13. *(34sts)*
Next row: cast off 4sts, p8, [k2, p3] twice, k2, p8, k1. *(30sts)*
Next row (dec row): k2, k2tog, k5, [p2, k3] twice, p2, k5, k2tog, k2. *(28sts)*
Next row: k1, p7, [k2, p3] twice, k2, p7, k1.
Keeping edge sts as st st, dec

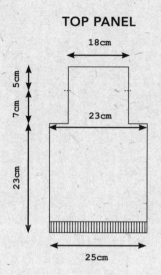

TOP PANEL

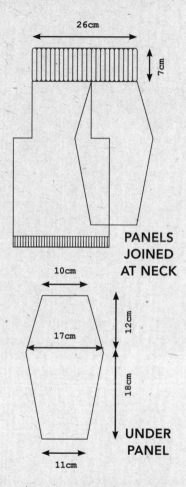

PANELS JOINED AT NECK

UNDER PANEL

by working 2sts together in this way on next and every 4th row until there are 18sts. Cont without shaping until leg hole measures 7cm. Place a marker at each edge

to mark where leg hole ends.
Cont straight in patt until work
matches top panel from leg hole,
ending with a ws row.

Joining the neck
Change to 4mm needles.
Next row (rs): [k2, p2] 4 times,
k2, then with rs facing, [p2, k2]
across the 40sts of the top panel
on the holder.
Work as set until rib measures
7cm, then cast off loosely in patt.

TO MAKE UP
Join the shoulder seams down
to marker, reversing seam on last
4cm of neck to fold over.
Leg hole border
With 4mm needles and rs facing,
pick up 30sts along the leg hole.
It doesn't matter if you pick up
more stitches, but do not pick
up fewer, and ensure you have
a number divisible by 4 plus 2.
Set rib patt
Next row (ws): [k2, p2] to last
2sts, k2.
Next row: [p2, k2] to last 2sts, p2.
Rep last 2 rows once more, then
the first row once again.
Cast off loosely in patt.
Repeat for the second leg.

Sew up the leg seams and then
sew the top panel to the under
panel, noting that the under
panel is shorter.
Weave in all loose ends.
Tip: This size of jumper has
a similar shape to that of
Italian Greyhounds.

🐾 FACT FILE

BEAR
....

Breed: Welsh Terrier.
Character: A true terrier, intensely focused one minute, easily distracted the next. Intelligent, alert, fun and very loyal.
Happiest When: Chasing rabbits in the spring sunshine; travelling to exciting places with his devoted owner, Verity.
Will Do Anything For: Peanut butter or Quavers.
Favourite Treat: Ice cream.
Hobbies Include: Travelling, digging up molehills and going to the pub.

Bear's Country Cable Jumper

I am fascinated by cables and the effects you can achieve with them and I love how the twists give a straightforward rib design a marvellous texture. The single rib adds a vintage feel that suits this handsome chap very well. This yarn is machine-washable, so your dog can get as grubby as he likes!

Size
Dog measurements
Neck 26–34cm
Shoulder 16–20cm
Chest 50–60cm
Length 44–47cm
See Measure Your Dog
 (page 79)

Garment measurements
Neck 24cm unstretched
Chest 46cm unstretched
Length 44cm plus collar

Yarn
2 x 100g balls of Rowan Pure
 Wool Worsted in Hazel 128

Needles and equipment
Pair of 4mm knitting needles
Cable needle
4 safety pins to use as markers
 for leg holes
Knitter's sewing needle

Tension
32sts and 29 rows over cable patt
 (slightly stretched) to a 10cm
 square using 4mm needles.

Abbreviations
See page 78.

TOP PANEL
Starting at the lower edge and with 4mm needles, cast on 61sts.
Set rib patt
Row 1 (rs): k2, [p1, k1] to last 3sts, p1, k2.
Row 2: k1, [p1, k1] to last 2sts, p1, k1.
Rep last 2 rows 4 times more.
Set cable patt
Row 1 (inc row) (rs): k5, [p3, k4] 7 times, p3, k3, M1, k1. *(62sts)*
Row 2: k1, [p4, k3] to last 5sts, p4, k1.
Row 3: k1, [C2F, C2B, p3] to last 5sts, C2F, C2B, k1.
Row 4: k1, [p4, k3] to last 5sts, p4, k1.
Row 5 (inc row): k1, M1, k4, [p3, k4] 7 times, p3, k4, M1, k1. *(64sts)*
Row 6: k1, p5, k3, [p4, k3] to last 6sts, p5, k1.
Row 7: k1, p1, [C2F, C2B, p3] to last 6sts, C2F, C2B, p1, k1.
Row 8: k2, [p4, k3] to last 6sts, p4, k2.
Rows 5–8 set cable patt with incs on every row 5. Work as set until there are 86sts, working the incs into the p3, k4 rib patt, and into the cable patt as enough stitches become available.
Then work straight (without incs) in patt until work measures approximately 25cm from cast on

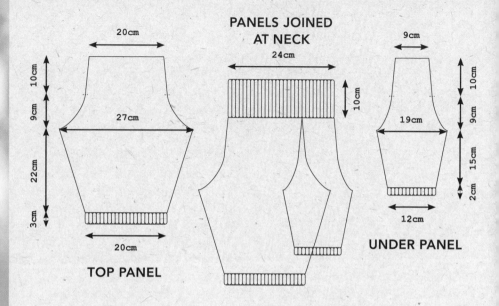

PANELS JOINED AT NECK

24cm

10cm

TOP PANEL

20cm

10cm

9cm

27cm

22cm

3cm

20cm

UNDER PANEL

9cm

10cm

9cm

19cm

15cm

2cm

12cm

edge, ending with row 8 (last row) of patt rep.

Shape leg

Keeping cable patt as set:

Next row (rs): cast off 3sts, p3, [k4, p3] to last 3sts, k3. *(83sts)*

Next row: cast off 3sts, k3, [p4, k3] to end. *(80sts)*

Next row (dec row): k1, p2tog, patt to last 3sts, p2tog, k1. *(78sts)*

Next row: k2, p4, [k3, p4] to last 2sts, k2.

Keeping cable and rib patt as set, dec by working 2sts together in patt, 1st in from each edge, on

the next row and every 4th row (row 5) of patt rep.

Cont to dec as set until there are 68sts. Cont without shaping until work measures approximately 34cm from cast on edge, ending with row 8 (last row) of patt rep.

Place a marker 9cm from start of leg shaping to mark top of leg hole.

Shape shoulder

Next row (rs): k1, k2tog, patt to last 3sts, k2tog, k1. *(66sts)*

Keeping cable and rib patt as set,

dec on every 4th row until there are 52sts. The work should now measure approximately 44cm from cast on edge.

Work 4 more rows of patt, dec by working 2sts together in patt, 1st in from each edge, on every row, work 1 row, then put these 44sts onto a stitch holder and set aside.

UNDER PANEL

Starting at the lower edge and with 4mm needles, cast on 36sts.

Set rib patt

Row 1 (rs): k3, [p2, k2] to last 5sts, p2, k3.

Row 2: k1, p2, [k2, p2] to last 5sts, k2, p2, k1.

These 2 rows set rib patt.

Cont in patt until rib measures 2cm from cast on edge, ending with a ws row.

Next row (inc row) (rs): k2, M1, k1, [p2, k2] to last 5sts, p2, k1, M1, k2. *(38sts)*

Next row: k1, p3, [k2, p2] to last 6sts, k2, p3, k1.

Keeping edge sts as st st, cont to inc on every 4th row as set until there are 48sts. Knit the first and last stitch on ws rows to give a neat edge.

Cont without shaping as set until work measures 17cm from cast on edge, ending with a ws row.

Leg shaping

Next row (rs): cast off 6sts, patt to end. *(42sts)*

Next row: cast off 6sts, patt to end. *(36sts)*

Next row (dec row): k2, k2tog, patt to last 4sts, k2tog, k2. *(34sts)*

Next row: k1, patt to last st, k1.

Keeping patt as set, dec on next and every 4th row until there are 26sts.

Cont straight, place a marker 9cm from start of leg shaping to mark top of leg hole, then cont straight until work matches top panel from leg hole, ending with a ws row.

Join the neck

With rs facing on under panel, set neck rib by working [k1, p1] across these 26sts, then with rs facing cont in rib across the 44sts of the top panel on the holder. Work in patt until rib measures 10cm, cast off loosely in patt.

TO MAKE UP

Block the top panel, and the sides of the under panel.

Sew up the shoulder seam from the bottom of the neck rib down to the markers at the top of the leg hole. For the other shoulder seam, turn the work inside out, and starting at the neck edge and using mattress stitch, sew 5cm of the seam, then turn work back to right side and finish the seam down to the markers at the top of the leg hole.

Leg hole border

With rs facing, pick up 41sts along the leg hole, from the leg shaping on the top panel, up to the shoulder seam and down to the start of the leg shaping on the under panel. It doesn't matter if you pick up more stitches, but do not pick up fewer, and ensure you have an odd number.

Set rib patt

Next row (ws): p1, [k1, p1] to end.

Next row: k1, [p1, k1] to end.

Rep last 2 rows 3 times more.

Cast off loosely in patt on ws.

Work second leg to match.

Sew up leg seams and then sew the top panel to the under panel.

🐾 FACT FILE

BRUNO

Breed: Whippet.
Character: A devoted companion, fond of treats, warm jumpers and comfy beds.
Happiest When: He has stolen any item of human food.
Will Do Anything For: Cheese.
Naughtiest Habit: Unlike Scout, the list is endless.
Favourite Treat: Dried fish skin, jerky, dried venison; the list goes on and on…
Hobbies Include: Chasing and catching his Frisbee or ball, sleeping under the sofa throw and barking at the treat cupboard door.

Bruno's Toasty Twisted Rib Jumper

This stitch pattern creates a mini-cable effect that isn't difficult to work; just mark off the rows as you complete them and once the pattern is established it is easy to follow. I have used a contrast colour for the under panel, neck and leg rib but it looks equally great in one colour.

Size
Dog measurements
Neck 26–32cm
Shoulder 19–22cm
Chest 60–72cm
Length 61–65cm
See Measure Your Dog (page 79)

Garment measurements
Neck 32cm unstretched
Chest 62cm unstretched
Length 55cm plus collar

Yarn
4 x 50g balls of Rowan Felted Tweed Aran in Flint (mc)
2 x 50g balls in Pebble (cc)

Needles and equipment
Pair each of 4mm and 5mm knitting needles
4 safety pins to use as markers for leg holes
1 stitch holder
Knitter's sewing needle

Tension
22sts and 26 rows over twisted rib patt to a 10cm square using 5mm needles.

Abbreviations
See page 78.

TOP PANEL
Starting at the lower edge with cc and 4mm needles, cast on 66sts.
Row 1 (rs): k4, [p2, k2] to last 6sts, p2, k4.
Row 2: k2, [p2, k2] to end.
These 2 rows set rib patt.
Change to mc.
Rep last 2 rows 4 times more.
Change to 5mm needles.
Set twisted rib patt
Row 1 (rs): knit.
Row 2: k2, [p2, k2] to end.
Row 3: p2, [T.2, p2] to end.
Row 4: k1, p to last st, k1.
These 4 rows set rib patt. Work these 4 rows once more.
Shape rump
Next row (inc row) (rs): k2, M1, k to last 2sts, M1, k2. *(68sts)*
Next row: k3, [p2, k2] to last 5sts, p2, k3.
Next row: k1, p2, [T.2, p2] to last 5sts, T.2, p2, k1.
Next row: k1, p to last st, k1.

Keeping twisted rib patt correct, inc as set on every alt row 1 (that is, every 8 rows) until there are 78sts, ending with patt row 4. Set new patt.

Row 1 (rs): knit.

Row 2: p2, [k2, p2] to end.

Row 3: k2, p2, [T.2, p2] to last 2sts, k2.

Row 4: k1, p to last st, k1.

Cont in patt as set until panel measures 33cm from cast on edge, finishing with patt row 4.

Shape leg

Next row (rs): cast off 4sts, k to end. (74sts)

Next row: cast off 4sts, p1, [k2, p2] to end. (70sts)

Work rows 3–4 of patt, keeping patt as set.

Next row (dec row): k2, k2tog, k to last 4sts, k2tog, k2. (68sts)

Next row: p1, [k2, p2] to last 3sts, k2, p1.

Next row: k1, p2, [T.2, p2] to last st, k1.

Next row: k1, p to last st, k1.

Dec as above on next and foll row 1 of patt rep. (64sts)

Cont in patt without shaping until leg hole measures 10cm, ending with patt row 4.

Place a marker at each end of row to mark bottom of leg hole.

Shape shoulder

Next row (dec row) (rs): k2, k2tog, knit to last 4sts, k2tog, k2. (62sts)

Work rows 2–4 of patt, keeping patt as set.

Dec as set on every patt row 1, keeping patt correct, until there are 50sts, and then work straight until panel measures 55cm from cast on edge.

Place these 50sts onto a stitch holder.

UNDER PANEL

Starting at the lower edge and with 4mm needles and cc, cast on 40sts.

Next row (rs): k3, [p2, k2] to last 5sts, p2, k3.

Next row: k1, p2, [k2, p2] to last 5sts, k2, p2, k1.

These 2 rows set rib patt.

Cont in patt until rib measures

TOP PANEL

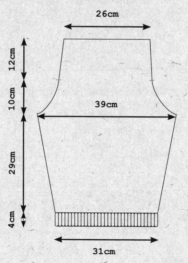

PANELS JOINED AT NECK

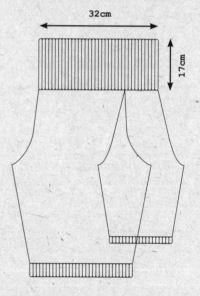

2cm from cast on edge, ending with a ws row.

Set twisted rib patt

Next row (inc row) (rs): k2, M1, k1, p2, [T.2, p2] to last 3sts, k1, M1, k2. *(42sts)*

Next row: k1, p3, [k2, p2] to last 6sts, k2, p3, k1.

Next row: k4, p2, [k2, p2] to last 4sts, k4.

Next row: k1, p3, [k2, p2] to last 6sts, k2, p3, k1.

Next row (inc row) (rs): k2, M1, k2, p2, [T.2, p2] to last 4sts, k2, M1, k2. *(44sts)*

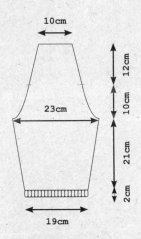

UNDER PANEL

These 4 rows set central twisted rib patt with st st borders. Knit the first st on every ws row to give a neat edge.

Keeping patt correct, inc and work into st st as set 2sts in from edge on every foll 8th row until there are 54sts.

Cont to work as set until panel measures 23cm from cast on edge, ending with a ws row.

Shape leg

Next row (rs): cast off 4sts, patt to end. *(50sts)*

Next row: cast off 4sts, patt to end. *(46sts)*

Next row (dec row): k2, k2tog, patt to last 4sts, k2tog, k2. *(44sts)*

Next row: work as patt.

Next row: dec, working k2tog as set. *(42sts)*

Cont in patt with no shaping until leg hole measures 10cm.

Place a marker at each end of row to mark top of leg hole.

Shape shoulder

Dec, working k2tog as above, on next and every alt row until there are 26sts.

Cont in patt with no shaping until under panel matches top panel from leg to shoulder seam, ending a ws row.

Join neck

With 4mm needles and mc, [p2, k2] across the 26 under panel sts, [p2, k2] the 50 top panel sts to last 2sts, k2. *(76sts)*

Cont in rib patt until neck rib measures 15cm.

Change to cc.

Cont in rib for a further 2cm.

Cast off loosely in patt.

TO MAKE UP

Join the shoulder seams down to the marker, turning the seam to the other side halfway down the neck rib so that the seam does not show when the neck is rolled down on the right side.

Leg hole border

With rs facing, 4mm needles and mc, pick up 42sts along the leg hole, from the leg shaping on the top panel, up to the shoulder seam and down to the beginning of the leg shaping on the under panel. It doesn't matter if you pick up more stitches, but do not pick up fewer, and ensure you have a number divisible by 4 plus 2.

Set rib patt

Next row (ws): [p2, k2] to last 2sts, p2.

Next row: [k2, p2] to last 2sts, k2.

Rep last 2 rows 8 times more.

Change to cc.

Work 2 more rows in rib.

Cast off loosely in patt.

Repeat for the second leg.

Sew up the side seams from the legs down; the under panel is 10cm shorter than the top panel.

Weave in all loose ends.

Tip: This jumper has been knitted in a variety of yarns and when knitted in DK it will come up smaller so do check your tension square to make necessary adjustments.

PIPPIN,
AKA PIPSQUEAK

Breed: Miniature Schnauzer.
Character: Busy, alert and happy. Loves to police the front garden from the sofa when left alone – a prohibited activity when family are home!
Happiest When: Off the lead on a walk. Also snorting and leaping around after a bath.
Will Do Anything For: Roast meat.
Naughtiest Habit: Waiting under the chopping board for a morsel to fall her way.
Favourite Treat: Peanut butter- and marmite-stuffed Kong toy.
Hobbies Include: Chasing squirrels and pigeons.

Pippin's Perfectly Pretty Coat

I discovered this stitch in a vintage pattern and I love it, especially done in this retro shade of pink. It is an easy stitch to work but requires concentration because it is tricky to unravel to make a correction. So mark off your rows and don't let anyone talk to you until a row is ticked off!

Size
Dog measurements
Neck 26–34cm
Shoulder 16–20cm
Chest 54–66cm
Length 41cm
See Measure Your Dog
   (page 79)

Garment measurements
Neck 24cm unstretched
Chest 45cm unstretched
Length 38cm plus collar

Yarn
2 x 100g balls of Rowan Pure
   Wool Worsted in Satin 116
(Note that this size takes all of 200g, so if you are adding any length you will need a third ball.)

Needles and equipment
Pair each of 4mm and 4.5mm
   knitting needles
4 stitch holders
Knitter's sewing needle
2 buttons

Tension
18sts and 22 rows over stitch
   patt to a 10cm square using
   4.5mm needles.

Abbreviations
See page 78.

MAIN PATTERN
Row 1 (rs): k2, [k1b, k1] to last st, k1.
Row 2: knit.
Row 3: [k1, k1b] to last st, k1.
Row 4: knit.
These 4 rows form patt rep.

TOP PANEL
Starting at the lower edge and with 4mm needles, cast on 90sts.
Row 1 (rs): k4, [p2, k2] to last 6sts, p2, k4.
Row 2: k2, [p2, k2] to end.
These 2 rows set rib patt. Cont in patt until rib measures 5cm from cast on edge, ending with row 1.
Next row (dec row): k2, [p2, k2] to last 12sts, p2tog, k2, p2, k2, p2, k2. *(89sts)*
Cut yarn.
Change to 4.5mm needles.
Next row: place 10sts onto a stitch holder, rejoin yarn, work main patt across next 69sts, place 10sts onto a stitch holder.

Work in patt across 69sts until work measures 38cm from cast on edge, ending with a ws row.

Divide for neck

Next row (rs): Patt across 19sts, place next 31sts on one stitch holder and the next 19sts on another stitch holder.

Next row: work in patt on these 19sts until panel measures 13cm from division of neck. Cast off.

Rejoin yarn to rem 19sts on stitch holder and rep from * to *.

Neck rib

With right side facing, pick up 26sts along right side of neck, knit across 31sts on stitch holder, pick up 25sts along left side of neck. (82sts)

Next row (ws): p2, [k2, p2] to end.

Next row: k2, [p2, k2] to end. These 2 rows set rib patt. Cont in patt until rib measures 10cm.

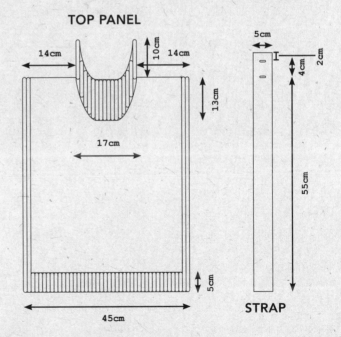

TOP PANEL

14cm — 10cm — 14cm

17cm

13cm

45cm

5cm

STRAP

5cm

2cm

4cm

55cm

Cast off loosely in patt.

Rib border

Put 10 edge sts on stitch holder on right side of coat onto 4mm needles and rejoin yarn.

*Next row (rs): k4, p2, k2, p2.

Next row: k2, p2, k2, p2, k2.

These 2 rows set rib patt. Cont in patt until, without stretching it, rib measures the same as the main panel. (You may find it easiest to sew the rib on as you work it to get the length right.) Cast off.*

Rejoin yarn to rem 10sts on stitch holder and rep from * to *.

STRAP

Using 4mm needles, cast on 10sts.

Row 1 (rs): k4, p2, k4.

Row 2: k2, p2, k2, p2, k2.

These 2 rows set strap rib patt. Cont in patt until strap measures 55cm from cast on edge, ending with a ws row. At this stage you can adjust strap length to suit your dog.

Next row: k4, yo, p2tog, k4.

Cont in patt until strap measures 59cm from cast on edge, ending with a ws row.

Next row: k4, yo, p2tog, k4.
Cont in patt until strap measures 61cm from cast on edge.
Cast off.

TO MAKE UP
Block main body panel and rib borders. Sew both rib borders to the top panel. Sew up the centre front seam. When you reach halfway up the neck, turn the seam to sew from the wrong side so that the seam does not show when the neck rib is rolled down. Position the strap across the middle of the top panel, with 11cm of the buttonhole side to the left of the coat, and sew on the strap securely through all layers at the centre top of the coat. Sew on buttons (I used two vintage ones) to other end of strap to align with buttonholes. Weave in all loose ends.

Textured Patchwork Blanket

Many dogs love the comfort of a warm blanket and this is a great project for using up all those odd balls of wool you might have stashed away in the cupboard! Two of the stitches used are featured in jumper projects and make for excellent practice if you are not a confident knitter.

Size
Finished blanket measures
 approximately 80 x 80cm

Yarn
2 x 100g balls of Rowan Pure
 Wool Worsted in each of
 Oats 152, Light Navy 153,
 Apple 129 and Bottle 140

Needles and equipment
Pair of 5mm knitting needles
Cable needle
Knitter's sewing needle

Tension
All tensions over patt to a 10cm
 square using 5mm needles.
Pattern 1: 17sts and 20 rows.
Pattern 2: 22sts and 30 rows.
Pattern 3: 21sts and 31 rows.
Pattern 4: 22sts and 32 rows.

Note that this blanket consists of four 20cm squares each of four different patterns; they all knit up slightly differently, so do check the measurements of each carefully to make sure that they are all the same size.

Abbreviations
See page 78.

PATTERN 1:
KNIT BELOW STITCH
Make 4 in Oats.
Note that Pattern 1 is very stretchy and you might have to cast on fewer sts to achieve 20cm, or go down a size to 4mm needles.
Mark the rows off as you knit as this pattern is hard to count, and very hard to unravel.
Cast on 35sts.
Knit one row.
Row 1 (rs): k2, [k1b, k1] to last st, k1.
Row 2: knit.
Row 3: [k1, k1b] to last st, k1.
Row 4: knit.
Rep rows 1–4 until work measures 20cm from cast on edge.
Cast off.

PATTERN 2:
FLAT CABLE
Make 4 in Light Navy.
Cast on 44sts.
Row 1 (rs): [p4, k4] to last 4sts, p4.
Row 2: [k4, p4] to last 4sts, k4.

Row 3: knit.
Row 4: purl.
Row 5: [k4, C4F] to last 4sts, k4.
Row 6: purl.
Rep rows 1–6 until work measures 20cm from cast on edge.
Cast off.

PATTERN 3:
TRICOLOUR FLAT RIB
Make 4 in Oats (mc), Apple (cc) and Bottle (cc2).
Cast on 41sts.
Row 1 (rs): mc knit.
Row 2: cc k2, [p2, k3] to last 4sts, p2, k2.
Row 3: cc2 knit.
Row 4: mc k2, [p2, k3] to last 4sts, p2, k2.
Row 5: cc knit.
Row 6: cc2 k2, [p2, k3] to last 4sts, p2, k2.
Rep rows 1–6, carrying the yarns not in use up the side, until work measures 20cm from cast on edge.
Cast off.

PATTERN 4:
TWISTED RIB
Make 2 in Apple and 2 in Bottle.
Cast on 42sts.
Row 1 (rs): knit.
Row 2: [p2, k2] to last 2sts, p2.
Row 3: k2, [p2, T.2] to last 4sts, p2, k2.
Row 4: purl.
Rep rows 1–4 until work measures 20cm from cast on edge.
Cast off.

TO MAKE UP
Block all the squares to the same size.
The blanket is 4 squares by 4 squares. To create the arrangement shown, sew them together using mattress stitch in the foll sequence:

Row 1
Pattern 3 : Pattern 2 : Pattern 1 : Pattern 4 in Bottle.
Row 2
Pattern 1 : Pattern 3 : Pattern 4 in Apple : Pattern 2.
Row 3
Pattern 2 : Pattern 4 in Apple : Pattern 3 : Pattern 1.
Row 4
Pattern 4 in Bottle : Pattern 1 : Pattern 2 : Pattern 3.

Then sew these rows together.

Patterns used in jumpers
Pattern 1 is used to make Pippin's Perfectly Pretty Coat, see page 32.
Pattern 4 is used to make Bruno's Toasty Twisted Rib Jumper, see page 26.
Tip: Try this blanket in one colour, it looks fantastic. If you are keen on crochet why not add a lovely border to finish off your blanket. Or, using an 80cm circular needle, you can pick up the stitches on each side, knit back and forth 3 rows, then cast off loosely to give a pretty knitted edge.

 FACT FILE

SCOUT, AKA
....
SCOUTY-PANTS
....

Breed: Whippet.
Character: A gentle, loyal chap, Scout is always by his human's side.
Happiest When: Chasing a ball – any ball.
Will Do Anything For: A ball.
Naughtiest Habit: His owner reports that he is perfect and has no naughty habits!
Favourite Treat: Food; if pushed for specifics, cheese.
Hobbies Include: Posing for his photographer owner even when there is no camera, finding and chasing balls and sleeping in a luxurious jumper.

Scout's Super-Snugly Jumper

This jumper is knitted in a beautifully soft yarn for a touch of luxury. It does require quite some concentration, but the moss stitch edge and cable design will keep you interested. I think a notebook is an asset when knitting this one!

Size
Dog measurements
Neck 26–32cm
Shoulder 19–22cm
Chest 60–72cm
Length 54–58cm
See Measure Your Dog
(page 79)

Garment measurements
Neck 29cm unstretched
Chest 60cm unstretched
Length 51cm plus collar

Yarn
3 x 50g balls of Yarn Stories Fine
Merino & Baby Alpaca Aran in
Toffee (mc)
1 x 50g ball in Taupe (cc)

Needles and equipment
Pair each of 3.5mm and 4mm
knitting needles
Cable needle
8 safety pins to use as markers
for leg holes
1 stitch holder
Knitter's sewing needle

Tension
23sts and 31 rows over st st to
a 10cm square using 4mm
needles.
The central cable and moss st
panel is 11.5cm wide.

Abbreviations
See page 78.

Notes
This jumper is knitted from the neck down, and the top panel and under panel are divided at the bottom of the neck rib and worked separately.

TOP PANEL
With cc and 3.5mm needles, cast on 70sts.
Next row (rs): knit.
Next row: purl.
Change to mc.
Next row: knit.
Set rib patt
Next row (ws): [k1, p3] to last 2sts, k2.
Next row: k1, p1, [k3, p1] to end.
These 2 rows set rib patt. Cont in patt until rib measures 11cm from cast on edge, ending with a ws row. Cut yarn.
Change to 4mm needles.
Divide sts to form under panel sts and top panel sts by putting the first 26sts onto a stitch holder for the under panel. Rejoin yarn

and work rem 44sts of top panel as folls:

Row 1 (rs): p1, [k1, p1] twice, k2, p1, k1, p1, [k6, p1, k1, p1] 3 times, k2, p1, [k1, p1] twice.

Row 2: p1, [k1, p1] twice, p3, k1, p1, [p6, p1, k1, p1] 3 times, p3, [k1, p1] twice.

Row 3 (cable & inc row): p1, [k1, p1] twice, k2, M1, p1, k1, p1, [k2, C4F, p1, k1, p1] 3 times, M1, k2, p1, [k1, p1] twice. *(46sts)*

Row 4: p1, [k1, p1] twice, p4, k1, p1, [p6, p1, k1, p1] 3 times, p4, [k1, p1] twice.

Row 5: p1, [k1, p1] twice, k3, p1, k1, p1, [k6, p1, k1, p1] 3 times, k3, p1, [k1, p1] twice.

Row 6: p1, [k1, p1] twice, p4, k1, p1, [p6, p1, k1, p1] 3 times, p4, [k1, p1] twice.

Row 7 (cable & inc row): p1, [k1, p1] twice, k3, M1, p1, k1, p1, [C4B, k2, p1, k1, p1] 3 times, M1, k3, p1, [k1, p1] twice. *(48sts)*

Row 8: p1, [k1, p1] twice, p5, k1, p1, [p6, p1, k1, p1] 3 times, p5, [k1, p1] twice.

These 8 rows set central cable and moss st patt panel with border edges of st st and 5 moss sts.

Cont in patt, inc and work into st st at outer edge of central panel on every 4th row as set until there are 60sts, at same time, when work measures 11cm from bottom of neck rib, place a marker at each end of row to mark top of leg hole.

Now inc as before but on every rs row until there are 84sts, at same time, when work measures 10cm from first markers, place a marker at each end of row to mark bottom of leg hole.

Cont as set straight for a further 12cm, ending on a ws row, then start to dec.

Next row (dec row): patt to 2sts before central cable and moss st patt panel, k2tog, patt 30, k2togtbl, patt to end. *(82sts)*

Next row: Patt to end.

Rep last 2 rows until there are 66sts.

Cont straight in patt until panel measures 45cm from bottom of neck rib, ending with a ws row, dec 1st in centre of last row. *(65sts)*

Moss stitch border

Change to 3.5mm needles.
Next row (rs): p1, [k1, p1] to end.
Rep last row until the border measures 6cm, ending with a ws row.
Change to cc.
Beg with a k row, work 3 rows st st.
Cast off on ws.

UNDER PANEL

Rejoin cc to 26sts on stitch holder at bottom of neck rib.
Next row (inc row) (rs): k1, [p1, k1] twice, [p1, k3] 4 times, p1, M1, [p1, k1] twice. *(27sts)*
Next row: [k1, p1] twice, k1, [k1, p3] 4 times, k2, [p1, k1] twice. This sets 17st central panel in k3, p1 rib with moss st border edges.

Shape chest

Next row (inc row): [k1, p1] twice, k1, M1, p1, [k3, p1] 4 times, M1, k1, [p1, k1] twice. *(29sts)*
Next row: [k1, p1] twice, k1, p1, [k1, p3] 4 times, k1, p1, k1, [p1, k1] twice.
Next row (inc row): [k1, p1]

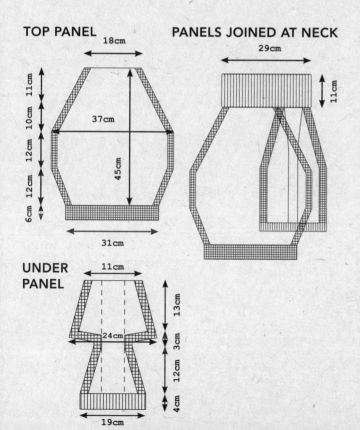

TOP PANEL
18cm
11cm
10cm
12cm
12cm
6cm
37cm
45cm
31cm

PANELS JOINED AT NECK
29cm
11cm

UNDER PANEL
11cm
13cm
3cm
12cm
4cm
24cm
19cm

twice, k2, M1, p1, [k3, p1] 4 times, M1, k2, [p1, k1] twice. (31sts)

Next row: [k1, p1] twice, k1, p2, [k1, p3] 4 times, k1, p2, k1, [p1, k1] twice.

Cont to inc and work into st st in this way at outer edges of central panel as set on every rs row until there are 49sts.

Cont in patt as set without shaping until work measures 10cm from bottom of neck rib, ending on a ws row.

For the next 8 rows work in moss st up to the central border as follows:

Next row (rs): moss st [k1, p1] 8 times, central panel [p1, k3] 4 times, p1, moss st [p1, k1] 8 times.

Next row (ws): moss st [k1, p1] 8 times, cental panel [k1, p3] 4 times, k1, moss st [p1, k1] 8 times.

Rep these 2 rows 6 times to give 8 rows of moss st with a central panel.

Shape leg

Next row (rs): cast off 10 sts, [p1, k1] twice, p1, central panel [p1, k3] 4 times, p1, [p1, k1] 8 times. (39sts)

Next row (ws): cast off 10 sts [p1, k1] twice, p1, central panel [k1, p3] 4 times, k1, [p1, k1] 3 times. (29sts)

Cont with the 6 moss sts at edge and central panel until work measures 16cm ending on a ws row.

Next row (rs): [k1, p1] 3 times, M1, p1 [k3, p1] 4 times, M1, [p1, k1] three times. (31sts)

Next row (ws): [k1, p1] 3 times, p1, [k1, p3] 4 times, k1, p1, [p1, k1] 3 times.

Cont to inc and work into st st in this way at outer edges of central panel, as set on every rs row until there are 47 sts – placing markers at edges 8cm from beginning of leg shaping to denote leg holes.

Cont in patt as set without shaping until work measures 32cm from bottom of neck rib, ending on a ws row.

Rib border

Change to 3.5mm needles.

Next row (rs): p1, k2, p1, [k3, p1] 10 times, k2, p1.

Next row (ws): k1, p2, k1, [p3, k1] 10 times, p2, k1.

Rep last 2 rows until rib measures 36cm from bottom of neck rib. Cast off loosely in patt.

TO MAKE UP

Block both panels gently, to avoid flattening the cable or rib. Sew up both shoulder seams from the beginning of the leg shaping at cast off row to the neck rib on one side, and all the way to the top of neck rib on the other. Then sew side seams from the leg markers to the bottom of the under panel, which should line up with the start of the final shaping on the top panel. Weave in all loose ends.

🐾 FACT FILE

DYLAN
....

Breed: Miniature Wire-Haired
Dachshund.
Character: Gentle, kind
and contented. Rescued at
just 6 months old, emaciated
and dehydrated he thrived
with love and care to live a
very happy life.
Happiest When: Digging for
his ball!
Will Do Anything For: Food.
Naughtiest Habit: Placing his
ball under the kitchen units
and talking non-stop at 5pm
every day!
Favourite Treat: Freshly
dug-up organic carrots.
Hobbies Include: Sleeping,
eating and ball-hiding.

Dylan's Dandy Rib Jumper

You produce this lovely stitch pattern by just purling every stitch on wrong side rows; it looks great on the reverse too, where the neck is turned back. The jumper has little garter stitch leg holes so it is more of a tank top and is ideal for short legs that love to dig.

Size
Dog measurements
Neck 22–28cm
Shoulder 12–15cm
Chest 38–44cm
Length 35–39cm
See Measure Your Dog
  (page 79)

Garment measurements
Neck 24cm unstretched
Chest 43cm unstretched
Length 33cm plus collar

Yarn
2 x 100g ball of Rowan Pure Wool
  Worsted in Grasshopper 130

Needles and equipment
Pair each of 4mm and 4.5mm
  knitting needles
6 safety pins to use as markers
  for leg holes
1 stitch holder
Knitter's sewing needle

Tension
22sts and 30 rows over patt to
  a 10cm square using 4.5mm
  needles.

Abbreviations
See page 78.

JUMPER
Starting at the neck edge and with 4mm needles, cast on 54sts.
Set rib patt
Row 1 (rs): [k2, p2] to last 2sts, k2.
Row 2: purl.
These 2 rows set rib patt. Cont in patt until rib measures 9cm from cast on edge, ending with a ws row.
Change to 4.5mm needles.
Next row (inc row): k1, M1, k1, [p2, k1, M1, k1] to end. *(68sts)*
Next row: purl.
Next row: [k3, p2] to last 3sts, k3.
Next row: purl.
The last 2 rows set new rib patt. Cont in patt until rib measures 15cm from cast on edge, ending with a ws row.
Place a marker on each edge at this point to mark top of leg shaping. Cut yarn.
Divide sts to form under panel sts and top panel sts by putting the first 20sts onto a stitch holder

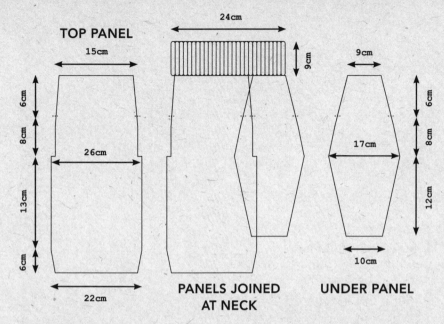

TOP PANEL

15cm

6cm

8cm

13cm

6cm

26cm

22cm

24cm

9cm

**PANELS JOINED
AT NECK**

9cm

6cm

8cm

17cm

12cm

10cm

UNDER PANEL

Work measures 42cm from cast on edge, ending with a ws row.
Knit one row.
Cast off knitwise on ws.

UNDER PANEL

With rs facing, rejoin yarn to 20sts on stitch holder.

Next row (inc row) (rs): k2, M1, k1, [p2, k3] 3 times, k2tog. (20sts)

Next row: purl.

Next row (inc row): k2, M1, k2, [p2, k3] twice, p2, k2, M1, k2. (22sts)

Next row: purl.

Cont to inc and work into st st on every rs row inside edge sts as set until there are 38sts.

Place marker at each end of row to mark bottom of leg hole.

Next row (dec row) (rs): k2, k2tog, k9, [p2, k3] twice, p2, k9, k2tog, k2.

Next row: purl.

Cont to dec on every rs row inside edge sts as set until there are 20sts.

Next row (rs): k4, p2, k3, p2, k3, p2, k4.

Next row: purl.

The last 2 rows set rib patt. Cont in patt until work measures 35cm

and work on the 48sts for the top panel. Rejoin yarn.

Next row (inc row): k1, M1, k2, [p2, k1, M1, k2] to end. (58sts)

Next row: purl.

Next row: [k4, p2] to last 4sts, k4.

Next row: purl.

The last 2 rows set new rib patt. Cont in patt until rib measures 8cm from where it was divided. Place a marker on each edge at this point to mark start of leg hole.

Cont in patt as set until work

measures 36cm from cast on edge, ending with a ws row.

Shape rump

Next row (rs): work 29sts, place a marker to mark the centre, work 29sts.

Next row: purl, slm, purl to end.

Next row (dec row): [k4, p2] 4 times, k3, k2tog, slm, k2tog, k3, [p2, k4] 4 times. (56sts)

Next row: purl, slm.

Cont to dec as set by last 2 rows (working k2tog on either side of the marker on every rs row) 7 times more. (42sts)

from cast on edge, ending with a ws row.
Knit one row.
Cast off knitwise on ws.

TO MAKE UP

Sew the under panel to the top panel from the neck to the first marker at top of leg hole shaping.

Leg hole border

With 4.5mm needles and rs facing, pick up 30sts along the top panel from the second marker at start of leg hole up to the seam and along the same point on the under panel.
Knit one row.
Cast off knitwise.
Work the second leg to match.
Sew up the side seams from the legs down.
Weave in all loose ends.

🐾 FACT FILE

NELLY

Breed: Miniature Schnauzer.
Character: Always on the go; always pleased to see anyone!
Happiest When: Barking her way down the street announcing her presence to all.
Will Do Anything For: Food – any kind of food.
Hobbies Include: Chasing cats, barking (a lot) and sliding into the paddling pool, but only during the summer months.
Favourite Treat: Dried venison bites.

Nelly's Properly Practical Coat

The item that inspired this little coat was a vintage Aran jumper bought in a French flea market. It is a challenging project for an experienced knitter. The result is a very smart little coat held in place around the front legs by the triangular under panel. It will fit small, straight-backed dogs.

Size
Dog measurements
Neck 26–34cm
Shoulder 16–20cm
Chest 54–66cm
Length 41cm
See Measure your Dog (page 79)

Garment measurements
Neck 32cm unstretched
Chest 52cm unstretched
Length 38cm plus collar

Yarn
2 x 100g balls of Rowan Pure Wool Worsted in Raspberry 117.
(3 balls if you need to knit it longer)

Needles and equipment
Pair each of 4.5mm and 5mm knitting needles
Cable needle
2 stitch markers
Knitter's sewing needle

Tension
25sts and 27 rows over patt to a 10cm square using 5mm needles.
The central panel is 12cm wide.

Abbreviations
See page 78.

TOP PANEL
Starting at the lower edge and with 4.5mm needles, cast on 89sts.
Row 1 (rs): [k1, p3] to last st, k1.
Row 2: [p1, k3] to last st, p1.
These 2 rows set rib patt. Cont in patt until rib measures 4cm from cast on edge, ending with a ws row.
Change to 5mm needles.
Set border patt and central panel
Next row (dec row) (rs): k2tog, [p1, k1] 3 times, [Tw2, p4] 3 times, Tw2, place marker, p2, k30, p2, place marker, Tw2, [p4, Tw2] 3 times, [k1, p1] 3 times, k1. *(88sts)*
Next row: k1, [p1, k1] 3 times, [p2, k4] 3 times, p2, slm, k2, p30, k2, slm, p2, [k4, p2] 3 times, [k1, p1] 3 times, k1.
Set trellis pattern into central panel
Row 1 (rs): k1, [p1, k1] 3 times, [Tw2, p4] 3 times, Tw2, slm, p2,

[Cr2f, p4, Cr1b] 3 times, p2, slm, Tw2, [p4, Tw2] 3 times, [k1, p1] 3 times, k1.

Row 2: k1, [p1, k1] 3 times, [p2, k4] 3 times, p2, slm, k3, [p2, k4, p2, k2] 3 times, k1, slm, p2, [k4, p2] 3 times, [k1, p1] 3 times, k1.

Row 3: k1, [p1, k1] 3 times, [Tw2, p4] 3 times, Tw2, slm, p3, [Cr2f, p2, Cr1b, p2] 3 times, p1, slm, Tw2, [p4, Tw2] 3 times, [k1, p1] 3 times, k1.

Row 4: k1, [p1, k1] 3 times, [p2, k4] 3 times, p2, slm, [k4, p2, k2, p2] 3 times, k4, slm, p2, [k4, p2] 3 times, [k1, p1] 3 times, k1.

Row 5: k1, [p1, k1] 3 times, [Tw2, p4] 3 times, Tw2, slm, [p4, Cr2f, Cr1b] 3 times, p4, slm, Tw2, [p4, Tw2] 3 times, [k1, p1] 3 times, k1.

Row 6: k1, [p1, k1] 3 times, [p2, k4] 3 times, p2, slm, [k5, p4, k1] 3 times, k4, slm, p2, [k4, p2] 3 times, [k1, p1] 3 times, k1.

Row 7: k1, [p1, k1] 3 times, [Tw2, p4] 3 times, Tw2, slm, [p5, C4B, p1] 3 times, p4, slm, Tw2, [p4, Tw2] 3 times, [k1, p1] 3 times, k1.

Row 8: k1, [p1, k1] 3 times, [p2, k4] 3 times, p2, slm, [k5, p4, k1] 3 times, k4, slm, p2, [k4, p2] 3 times, [k1, p1] 3 times, k1.

Row 9: k1, [p1, k1] 3 times, [Tw2, p4] 3 times, Tw2, slm, [p4, Cr1b, Cr2f] 3 times, p4, slm, Tw2, [p4, Tw2] 3 times, [k1, p1] 3 times, k1.

Row 10: k1, [p1, k1] 3 times, [p2, k4] 3 times, p2, slm, [k4, p2, k2, p2] 3 times, k4, slm, p2, [k4, p2] 3 times, [k1, p1] 3 times, k1.

Row 11: k1, [p1, k1] 3 times, [Tw2, p4] 3 times, Tw2, slm, p3, [Cr1b, p2, Cr2f, p2] 3 times, p1, slm, Tw2, [p4, Tw2] 3 times, [k1, p1] 3 times, k1.

Row 12: k1, [p1, k1] 3 times, [p2, k4] 3 times, p2, slm, k3, [p2, k4, p2, k2] 3 times, k1, slm, p2, [k4, p2] 3 times, [k1, p1] 3 times, k1.

Row 13: k1, [p1, k1] 3 times, [Tw2, p4] 3 times, Tw2, slm, p2, [Cr1b, p4, Cr2f] 3 times, p2, slm, Tw2, [p4, Tw2] 3 times, [k1, p1] 3 times, k1.

Row 14: k1, [p1, k1] 3 times, [p2, k4] 3 times, p2, slm, k2, [p2, k6, p2] 3 times, k2, slm, p2, [k4, p2] 3 times, [k1, p1] 3 times, k1.

Row 15: k1, [p1, k1] 3 times, [Tw2, p4] 3 times, Tw2, slm, p2, k2, [p6, C4F] twice, p6, k2, p2, slm, Tw2, [p4, Tw2] 3 times, [k1, p1] 3 times, k1.

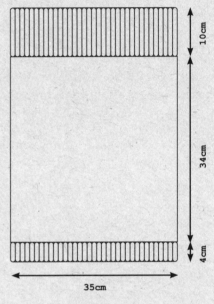

10cm
34cm
4cm
35cm

TOP PANEL

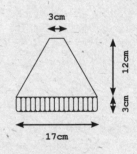

3cm
12cm
3cm
17cm

UNDER PANEL

Row 16: k1, [p1, k1] 3 times, [p2, k4] 3 times, p2, slm, k2, [p2, k6, p2] 3 times, k2, slm, p2, [k4, p2] 3 times, [k1, p1] 3 times, k1. These 16 rows set trellis patt in central panel. Cont in patt until work measures approximately 38cm from cast on edge, ending with either row 8 or row 16 of patt rep.

Neck rib

Change to 4.5mm needles.

Next row (dec row) (rs): [k3, p1] to last 4sts, k2, k2tog. *(87sts)*

Next row: [p3, k1] to last 3sts, p3.

Next row: [k3, p1] to last 3sts, k3. The last 2 rows set rib patt. Cont in patt until rib measures 10cm, then cast off loosely in patt. Sew the neck seam, starting on the rs, then turning to the ws halfway down so that the seam does not show when the neck is rolled down.

UNDER PANEL

With 4.5mm needles and rs of body facing, pick up 7sts across bottom of neck seam, starting 1cm down from seam on one side and picking up across to 1cm down on the other side.

Next row: k1, p5, k1
Next row: knit.
Next row: k1, p5, k1.
Change to 5mm needles.
Next row (inc row) (rs): k2, M1, k3, M1, k2. *(9sts)*
Next row: k1, p7, k1.
The last 2 rows set incs in patt. Cont to inc as set until there are 37sts, ending with a ws row.
Rib border
Next row: [k1, p3] to last st, k1.
Next row: [p1, k3] to last st, p1.
The last 2 rows set rib patt. Cont in patt until rib measures 3cm, then cast off loosely in patt.

TO MAKE UP
Block both panels gently. Right sides together, fold the under panel flat against the top panel and, starting at the cast off edge of the under panel, sew each end of the rib section to the sides of the top panel.
Tip: You can knit this coat longer if your dog needs it, just keep going with the pattern until you reach the length you need but try and finish on a row 8 or 16 to keep it neat.

🐾 FACT FILE

FRANKIE
....

Breed: Lurcher (Whippet/
Saluki cross).
Character: Gentle, kind and
loved by all. Scared of her
own shadow and anything
that makes a loud bang.
Happiest When: Chasing
squirrels.
Will Do Anything For:
Venison chews.
Naughtiest Habit: Creeping
upstairs after lights out and
messing up the spare bed to
get comfy for the night.
Favourite Treat: Chicken,
freshly roasted.
Hobbies Include: Sleeping,
begging for toast and barking
at cats.

Frankie's Super Sloppy Joe Jumper

I love knitting in the round because you are always looking at the right side, there are very few seams to sew up and it really isn't difficult to do. The double moss stitch pattern looks great in this Aran-weight yarn and the shaping gives this jumper a lovely fit around the neck and shoulders.

Size

Dog measurements
Neck 36–40cm
Shoulder 28cm
Chest 71–75cm
Length 66–69cm
See Measure Your Dog
  (page 79)

Garment measurements
Neck 30cm unstretched
Chest 69cm unstretched
Length 61cm plus collar

Yarn
4 x 100g balls of Wendy
  Traditional Aran in Grouse 191

Needles and equipment
One each of 40cm 4.5mm and
  80cm 5mm circular needle
Set of 4 x 4mm double-pointed
  needles
4 stitch markers
3 stitch holders
Knitter's sewing needle

Tension
18sts and 28 rows over double
  moss patt to a 10cm square
  using 5mm needles.

Abbreviations
See page 78.

Notes
This jumper is knitted for the
  most part in the round on a
  circular needle, and the pattern
  assumes that the rs is the inside
  of the knitting.

JUMPER
Starting at the neck edge and
with 4mm circular needle, cast
on 72sts. Ensuring that the work
is not twisted, place marker and
join the round.
Round 1: [k2, p2] to end.
This row sets rib patt. Cont in
patt until rib measures 2cm, then
change to 5mm circular needle
and cont until rib measures 15cm
(or length of dog's neck) from
cast on edge.
Divide sts to form back sts, first
leg sts, chest sts and second leg
sts as folls:
Next round: working in k2, p2,
rib throughout, rib across 22sts
for back, place marker, rib across

18sts for first leg, place marker, rib across 14sts for chest, place marker, rib across 18sts for second leg.

Set double moss back panel and rib patt

Next round: [k2, p2] across back sts to last 2sts, k2, slm, rib as set across first leg, chest and second leg sts, slm.

Next round: [k2, p2] across back sts to last 2sts, k2, slm, rib as set across first leg, chest and second leg sts, slm.

Next round: [p2, k2] across back sts to last 2sts, p2, slm, rib as set across first leg, chest and second leg sts, slm.

Next round: [p2, k2] across back sts to last 2sts, p2, slm, rib as set across first leg, chest and second leg sts, slm.

Shape shoulder

Next round (inc round): k1, M1, k1, [p2, k2] across back sts to last 4sts, p2, k1, M1, k1, slm, rib as set across first leg, chest and second leg sts, slm.

Inc back sts on every round in this way (working 1st in patt, making a stitch, working in patt to 1st before marker, making a stitch,

working last st in patt), taking incs into double moss patt, until there are 92sts on the back panel (35 inc rounds worked).

Cont in patt with no further incs until work measures 19cm from the bottom of rib: check that from centre back neck diagonally down to edge measures 28cm (dog's shoulder length).

Make leg holes
Next round: work back sts in patt, rib across 18 first leg sts then put them onto a stitch holder, rib across 14 chest sts, rib across 18 second leg sts then put them onto a stitch holder.
Next round: work back sts in patt, cast on 18sts for first leg, rib across 14 chest sts, cast on

18sts for second leg, ensuring the markers are in place again. Cont to knit in the round in patt as set until work measures 43cm from bottom of neck rib.
Shape under chest
Next round (dec round): work back sts in patt, rib across first leg sts to 1st before marker, slip next st onto rh needle, remove

BACK

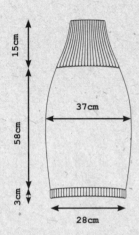

15cm

58cm

3cm

37cm

28cm

FRONT

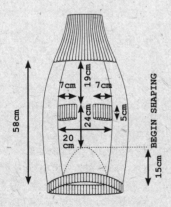

58cm

7cm 19cm 7cm

24cm 5cm

20 cm

BEGIN SHAPING

15cm

marker and slip st back onto lh needle, k2tog, rib across chest sts to 1st before marker, slip next st onto rh needle, remove marker and slip st back onto lh needle, k2tog, rib across second leg sts. Cont to dec as set on every round, altering the dec made (either k2tog or p2tog) to suit patt, until all 18sts of each leg are eliminated. Under panel should now measure approximately 48cm from bottom of neck rib.

Next round: work back sts in patt as set, rib across 14 chest sts then put them onto a stitch holder. Work back sts, working back and forth on the circular needle.

Shape rump

Next row (dec row) (rs): k2, k2tog, work in patt as set to last 4sts, k2tog, k2.

Next row: work in patt as set. Cont to dec as set on every rs row, working the dec 2sts in from the edge, altering the dec made (k2tog or p2tog) to suit patt, until you have 68sts and the work measures approximately 58cm.

Rib border

Turn work to rs out. With rs facing and 4mm circular needle, knit in pattern across the back 68sts, then pick up 19sts down the first side, knit across the 14 chest sts, then pick up 19sts down the other side of the top panel to complete the round.

Place marker and commence working in the round.

Next round: [k2, p2] to end.
Rep last round 5 times more.
Cast off loosely in patt.

LEG HOLE BORDER

With rs facing and 4mm dpns, pick up 18sts along cast off edge of leg hole, then rib the 18sts from the stitch holder.
Place a marker at beg of round.
Round 1: [k2, p2] to end.
Rep this round 11 times more.
Cast off loosely in patt.
Repeat for second leg hole border.

TO MAKE UP

Weave in all loose ends.
Tip: If you don't fancy the moss stitch just knit the back stitches – this looks particularly good in a mult-coloured yarn, giving the effect of stripes.
Try on your dog as you knit to check the fit, adjusting if you need to.

🐾 FACT FILE

EDIE
·················

Breed: Bedlington Terrier.
Character: Funny, happy, inquisitive little dog; very easily distracted!
Happiest When: She has an audience!
Will Do Anything For: Dried fish skins.
Naughtiest Habit: Barking at dogs on the television.
Favourite Treat: Prawn crackers and sausages.
Hobbies Include: Watching tennis and noisily dropping her toys from the sofa onto the floor.

Edie's Robust Romp-Around Jumper

This pattern is so easy to work, just a simple combination of knits and purls, yet the effect will leave you feeling a great sense of achievement by the end. I have chosen two colours that are perfect for Edie, but the texture would work well with just one colour.

Size

Dog measurements
Neck 26–34cm
Shoulder 16–20cm
Chest 54–66cm
Length 48–51cm
See Measure Your Dog
  (page 79)

Garment measurements
Neck 24cm unstretched
Chest 52cm unstretched
Length 44cm plus collar

Yarn

2 x 50g skeins of Erika Knight
  Vintage Wool in Drizzle (mc)
1 x 50g skein in Flax (cc)

Needles and equipment

Pair each of 4mm and 4.5mm
  knitting needles
4 safety pins to use as markers
  for leg holes
1 stitch holder
Knitter's sewing needle

Tension

19sts and 30 rows over ridge and
  stripe patt to a 10cm square
  using 4.5mm needles.

Abbreviations

See page 78.

TOP PANEL

Starting at the lower edge and with 4mm needles and cc, cast on 54sts.
Row 1 (rs): k4, [p2, k2] to last 6sts, p2, k4.
Row 2: k2, [p2, k2] to end.
These 2 rows set rib patt.
Change to mc.
Rep last 2 rows 5 times more, dec 1st at beg of last row. *(53sts)*
Change to 4.5mm needles.
Change to cc.
Row 1 (rs): knit.
Row 2: k1, p to last st, k1.
Change to mc.
Row 3: knit.
Row 4: k1, p to last st, k1.
Row 5: knit.
Row 6: k1, p to last st, k1.
Row 7: k1, p to last st, k1.
Row 8: k1, [p1, k1] to end.
These 8 rows form ridge and stripe patt, which is repeated throughout the panel.

Shape rump

Next row (inc row): k2, M1, k to last 2sts, M1, k2. *(55sts)*
Work rows 2–4 of patt.
Next row (inc row): k2, M1, k to last 2sts, M1, k2. *(57sts)*
Work rows 6–8 of patt.
Cont in patt, increasing on rows 1 and 5 as set, until there are 65sts.
Cont in patt without shaping until work measures 25cm from cast on edge, ending with row 8 of patt.

Shape leg

Keeping ridge and stripe patt correct:
Next row: cast off 4sts, k to end. *(61sts)*
Next row: cast off 4sts, p to last st, k1. *(57sts)*
Next row (dec row): k2, k2tog, k to last 4sts, k2tog, k2. *(55sts)*
Next row: k1, p to last st, k1.
Work rows 5–8 of patt.
Next row (dec row): k2, k2tog, k to last 4sts, k2tog, k2. *(53sts)*
Work rows 2–4 of patt.
Next row (dec row): k2, k2tog, k to last 4sts, k2tog, k2. *(51sts)*
Work rows 6–8 of patt.
Cont in patt without shaping until work measures approximately 34cm from cast on edge, ending

with row 2, 4 or 8 of patt, at the same time leg hole measures 9cm from start of shaping, place marker at each end of row to mark top of leg hole.

Shape shoulder

Next row (dec row) (rs): k2, k2tog, k to last 4sts, k2tog, k2. *(49sts)*
Next row: k1, p to last st, k1.
Cont to dec on every 4th row until there are 45sts. Cont in patt until panel measures 44cm from cast on edge, ending with row 2 of patt, dec 1st in centre of last

row. Put these 44sts onto a stitch holder and set aside.

UNDER PANEL

Starting at the lower edge and with 4.5mm needles and mc, cast on 36sts.
Row 1 (rs): k3, [p2, k2] to last 5sts, p2, k3.
Row 2: k1, p2, [k2, p2] to last 5sts, k2, p2, k1.
These 2 rows set rib patt. Cont in patt until rib measures 2cm from cast on edge, ending with a ws row.

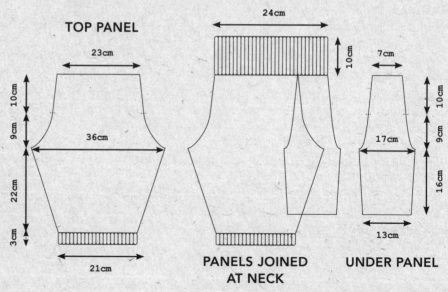

TOP PANEL

23cm

10cm

9cm

22cm

3cm

36cm

21cm

24cm

10cm

PANELS JOINED AT NECK

UNDER PANEL

7cm

10cm

9cm

16cm

17cm

13cm

Shape tummy
Next row (inc row) (rs): k2, M1, k1, [p2, k2] to last 5sts, p2, k1, M1, k2. *(38sts)*

Next row: k1, p3, [k2, p2] to last 6sts, k2, p3, k1.

Keeping 2 edge sts as st st, cont in patt, inc on every 4th row as set until there are 48sts. Knit the first and last stitch on ws rows to give a neat edge.

Cont without shaping until work measures 16cm from cast on edge, ending with a ws row.

Shape leg
Next row (rs): cast off 6sts, patt to end. *(42sts)*

Next row: cast off 6sts, patt to end. *(36sts)*

Next row (dec row): k2, k2tog, patt to last 4sts, k2tog, k2. *(34sts)*

Next row: k1, patt to last st, k1.

Keeping patt as set, dec on next and every 4th rs row until there are 26sts.

Place a marker at each end of the row when leg hole measures 9cm from start of shaping.

Cont straight until work matches top panel from leg hole marker, ending with a ws row.

Join the neck

With mc and rs facing on under panel, [k2, p2] 6 times, k2 across these 26sts, then with rs facing cont the rib as set across the 44sts of the top panel on the stitch holder. (70sts)

Work in patt until rib measures 9cm.

Cut mc and join in cc.

Work 2 rows in patt.

Cast off loosely in patt.

TO MAKE UP

Sew up the shoulder seam from the bottom of the neck rib down to the markers at the top of the leg hole.

For the other shoulder seam, turn the work inside out, and starting at the neck edge and using mattress stitch, sew 5cm of the seam, then turn work back to right side and finish the seam down to the markers at the top of the leg hole.

Leg hole border

With rs facing, mc and 4mm needles, pick up 34sts along the leg hole, from the leg shaping on the top panel, up to the shoulder seam and down to the start of the leg shaping on the under panel. It doesn't matter if you pick up more stitches, but do not pick up fewer, and ensure you have a number divisible by 4 plus 2.

Set rib patt

Next row (ws): [p2, k2] to last 2sts, p2.

Next row: [k2, p2] to last 2sts, k2.

Rep last 2 rows 3 times more.

Cut mc and join in cc.

Work 2 rows in patt.

Cast off loosely in patt.

Work the second leg to match.

Sew up the leg seams and then sew the top panel to the under panel, noting that the under panel is shorter.

Tip: The neck, shoulder and chest will fit a small whippet – just knit the back and under panel to the required length. You will need at least two more skeins of wool in the main colour.

🐾 FACT FILE

GLADYS

Breed: Italian Greyhound.
Character: Lively, bouncy and cuddly, with a naughty side.
Happiest When: Being chased and not being caught!
Will Do Anything For: Cuddles and kisses.
Naughtiest Habit: Burying her dinner in the sofa and investigating the cat litter tray…
Favourite Treat: Almonds and tea.
Hobbies Include: Snoozing in a comfy bed and munching on a rawhide chew.

Gladys's Roomy Raglan Jumper

Cable patterns were a challenge I was determined to master and with some tuition I have learnt to embrace this wonderful way of knitting texture. The cable in this pattern is a simple one, ideal for someone new to cables. The raglan sleeve gives your hound plenty of room to run around in.

Size
Dog measurements
Neck 25–30cm
Neck Length 8cm
Shoulder 12–13cm
Chest 40–50cm
Length 34cm
See Measure Your Dog
  (page 79)

Garment measurements
Neck 22cm unstretched
Chest 36cm unstretched
Length 35cm plus collar

Yarn
2 x 50g balls of Yarn Stories
  Fine Merino & Baby Alpaca DK
  Colour Cobalt
Or 2 x 50g balls of Willow & Lark,
  cashmere, merino, viscose mix

Needles and equipment
Pair each of 3.5mm and 4mm
  knitting needles
Set of 4 x 3.5mm double-pointed
  needles
Cable needle
2 stitch markers
2 stitch holders
Knitter's sewing needle

Tension
22sts and 30 rows over cable patt
  (unstretched) to a 10cm square
  using 4mm needles.

Abbreviations
See page 78.

CABLE PATT (40 STS)
Row 1 (rs): [k4, p2] rep to last 4 sts, k4.
Row 2 (ws): [p4, k2] rep to last 4sts, p4.
Row 3 (cable row): [C4F, p2, C4B] rep to last 4sts, C4F.
Row 4: as row 2.
Row 5: as row 1.
Row 6: as row 2.
Row 7: as row 1.
Row 8: as row 2.
Row 9 (cable row): [C4B, p2, C4F] rep to last 4sts, C4B.
Row 10: as row 2.
Row 11: as row 1.
Row 12: as row 2.
Row 13: as row 1.
Row 14: as row 2.
Row 15: as row 1.
Row 16: as row 2.
These 16 rows create the cable patt and are repeated on the 40sts of the top panel and the middle sts if the under panel throughout the length of the jumper.

JUMPER

Starting at the neck edge
and with 3.5mm needles, cast
on 78sts.

Next row (rs): [k4, p2] to last
4sts, k4.

Next row: [p4, k2] to last 4sts, p4.
These 2 rows set rib patt. Cont in
patt until rib measures 6cm from
cast on edge, ending with a ws
row. Cut yarn.

Change to 4mm needles.

Divide Top Panel and Under Panel:

Put the first 22sts onto a Stitch
holder (these sts will be your
under panel and we will return to
them later).

Rejoin yarn and the Top Panel
worked as follows over the rem
56 sts.

Next row (rs): k6 *(1st legs sts)*,
place marker, work row 1 of cable
patt, place marker, p2, place
marker, k6 *(2nd leg sts)*.*(56 sts)*

Next row: p6, slm, k2, slm,
work row 2 of cable patt, slm,
k2, slm, p6.

Next row: Start leg inc k1, M1,
k4, M1, k1, slm, p2, slm, work row
3 of cable patt (cable row), slm,
p2, slm, k1, M1, k4, M1, k1. *(60 sts)*

FINISHED GARMENT

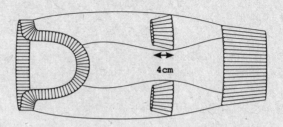

4cm

PANELS JOINED AT NECK

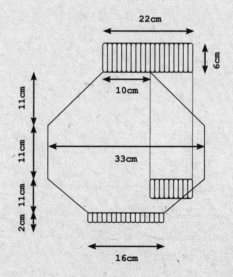

22cm

6cm

10cm

11cm

11cm

11cm

2cm

33cm

16cm

Next row: p8, slm, k2, slm, work row 4 of cable patt, slm, k2, slm, p8.

Next row: k1, M1, k6, M1, k1, slm, p2, slm, work Row 5 of cable patt, slm, p2, slm, k1, M1, k6, M1, k1. *(64 sts)*

Next row: p10, slm, k2, slm, work Row 6 of cable patt, slm, k2, slm, p10.

Next row: k1, M1, k8, M1, k1, slm, p2, slm, work row 7 of cable patt, slm, p2, slm, k1, M1, k8, M1, k1. *(68 sts)*

Next row: p12, slm, k2, slm, work row 8 of cable patt, slm, k2, slm, p12.

Next row: k1, M1, k10, M1, k1, slm, p2, slm, work Row 9 of cable patt, slm, p2, slm, k1, M1, k10, M1, k1. *(72 sts)*

Next row: p14, slm, k2, slm, work Row 10 of cable patt, slm, k2, slm, p14.

Next row: k1, M1, k12, M1, k1, slm, p2, slm work Row 11 of cable patt, slm, p2, slm, k1, M1, k12, M1, k1. *(76 sts)*

Next row: p16, slm, k2, slm, work row 12 of cable patt, slm, k2, slm, p16.

Next row: k1, M1, k14, M1, k1, slm, p2, slm, work Row 13 of cable patt, slm, p2, slm, k1, M1, k14, M1, k1. *(80 sts)*

Next row: p18, slm, k2, slm, work Row 14 of cable patt, slm, k2, slm, p18.

Next row: k1, M1, k16, M1, k1, slm, p2, slm, work Row 15 of cable patt, slm p2, slm, k1, M1, k16, M1, k1. *(84 sts)*

Next row: p20, slm, k2, slm, work row 16 of cable patt, slm, k2, slm, p20.

Next row (rs): k1, M1, k18, M1, k1, slm, p2, slm, work Row 1 of cable patt slm, p2, slm, k1, M1, k8, M1, k1. *(88sts)*
(22 sts for each leg, 40 sts cable patt, p2 x 2 between the leg sts and cable patt)

Next row (ws): p22, slm, k2, slm, work Row 2 of cable patt, slm, k2, slm, p22.

Cont to work in patt as set with no more inc until you have completed the whole 16 row cable patt repeat. the work should measure 11 cms.

Divide for legs

Next row (rs): Place the first leg sts onto a piece of contrasting yarn, cut off yarn and then rejoin it to work as follows on the same row. P2, work row 1 of cable patt, place the second leg sts onto a piece of contrasting yarn, while still on this row with rs facing re-cast on 20sts. NB this is so the rib pattern lines up. When picking up the leg stitches later on you will be picking up 22sts over the 20sts cast off edge.

Next row: p8, k2, p4, k2, p4, k2, work Row 2 of cable patt, cast on 20 sts for other leg. Again this is so the rib patt lines up. See the note above.

Next row: k8, p2, k4, p2, k4, p2, work Row 3 of cable patt, p2, k4, p2, k4, p2, k8.

Next row: keeping patt as set

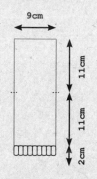

9cm

11 cm

11 cm

2 cm

UNDER PANEL

keep knitting and on the next cable row (row 9) include the new rib sts but not the edge 8 sts, these stay as st st.
Cont until work measures 11cm from the leg hole making a note of which row you are on, then start side shaping.

Next row: k2, k2tog, patt to last 4sts, k2, k2tog. *(82sts)*
Work one ws row in patt
Next row: repeat the decrease as above. *(80sts)*
Cont to knit in patt decreasing every rs row 2 sts in from each edge until you have 52sts and work measures 33cm from bottom of neck rib.
Keep these 52sts on a stitch holder.
Return to the under panel sts and with 4mm needles and rs facing
Row 1: (k4, p2) 3 times, k4.
Row 2: (p4, k2) 3 times, p4.
Row 3: k4, p2, C4B, p2, C4F, p2, k4.
Row 4: as row 2.
Row 5: as row 1.
Row 6: as row 2.
Row 7: as row 1.
Row 8: as row 2.

Row 9: k4, p2, C4F, p2, C4B, p2, k4.
Row 10: as row 2.
Rows 11–16: rep rows 1 and 2, 3 times more.
Cont in this patt until work measures 22cm, matching the beginning of the side shaping of top panel, placing a marker at 11cm to denote the leg opening. Put these 22sts onto a stitch holder.

TO MAKE UP
Lay out the knitting and block the edges gently to the measurements required.
Sew the top panel to the under panel along the left seam from the bottom up, taking care to match the leg opening with the marker on the under panel. Rep for other side.
Rib border
With rs facing and 3.5mm dpns, [k4, p2] pick up 20sts along the left top panel shaped edge, rib across the top panel sts, [k4, p2] then pick up 20sts along the right side top panel shaped edge to complete the round. *(114sts)*

Place marker and commence working in the round.
Next row (ws): [p4, k2] to last 4sts, p4.
Nest row (rs): [k4, p2] to last 4sts, k4.
Work these 2 rows for 2cm then cast off loosely rib wise.
Sew up the rem seam from the rib edge up to the neck edge, taking care to match the leg opening with the marker on the under panel.
Leg hole border
With rs facing and 3.5mm dpns, pick up 22sts along cast off edge of leg hole, then knit the 22sts from the waste yarn. *(44sts)*
Place a marker at beg of round.
Round 1: [k2, p2] to end.
Rep this round until leg measures 4cm.
Cast off loosely in patt.
Work second leg hole border to match.
Weave in all loose ends.
Tip: This jumper looks lovely with a contrast colour on the neck and body rib, but you will need this as an extra ball to the two balls in the main colour, as one of the main colour is not quite sufficient.

Abbreviations

alt alternate

C2(4)(6)B Cable 2(4)(6) back: slip the next stitch (2 stitches) (3 stitches) onto a cable needle and hold at back of work, knit the next stitch (2 stitches) (3 stitches) on the left-hand needle, then knit the stitch (2 stitches) (3 stitches) from the cable needle.

C2(4)(6)F Cable 2 (4) (6) front: slip the next stitch (2 stitches) (3 stitches) onto a cable needle and hold at front of work, knit the next stitch (2 stitches) (3 stitches) on the left-hand needle, then knit the stitch (2 stitches) (3 stitches) from the cable needle.

cc contrast colour

cont continue(ing)

Cr1b Cross 1 back: slip the next stitch onto a cable needle and hold at back of work, knit the next 2 stitches on the left-hand needle, then purl the stitch from the cable needle.

Cr2f Cross 2 front: slip the next 2 stitches onto a cable needle and hold at front of work, purl the next stitch on the left-hand needle, then knit the 2 stitches from the cable needle.

dec(s) decrease(s)/decreasing

dpn(s) double-pointed needle(s)

foll(s) follow(s)/following

inc(s) increase(s)/increasing

k knit

k1b knit 1 below: insert right needle into next stitch one row below and knit.

k2tog knit 2 stitches together.

lh left hand

M1 make a stitch: from the front pick up the bar between the last stitch worked and the next stitch, place it on the left-hand needle and knit into the back of it.

mc main colour

p purl

p2tog purl 2 stitches together.

patt pattern

rem remain(ing)

rep repeat

rh right hand

rs right side

slm slip marker(s)

st(s) stitch(es)

st st stocking stitch

T.2 knit two stitches together, don't slip them off the left-hand needle, then knit into the first stitch again and slip both original stitches off the left-hand needle.

tbl work through the back of the stitch, not the front.

tog together

Tw2 knit into the second stitch on the left-hand needle and lift it over the first stitch, then knit into the first stitch as normal.

ws wrong side

yo yarn over

Measure Your Dog

Dogs come in a variety of sizes within their breed groups. Before you start knitting it's a good idea to measure your dog to compare against our guide measurements for each project.

The most important measurements are:

A Neck: this will enable you to decide if you need more stitches in the neck rib, as ideally the rib needs to be relaxed when sitting on the dog's neck, and must stretch over the head to put the jumper on.

B Length: measure from the base of your dog's neck along the spine to where you want the jumper to end. Most of the jumpers are designed to be at least 10cm from the top of the tail, but the coats are designed to go all the way to the top of the tail.

C Shoulder: this is important to obtain a good fit. Measure from the centre of your dog's neck – where the collar sits at the top of the spine – diagonally down to the top of the leg, and do the same with your knitting (see diagram). By getting this

measurement right, the jumper will not pull back or slouch forward, but will fit comfortably on the dog.

D Chest: measure all the way around your dog's chest, just behind the front legs. This will tell you if you need to add in some stitches before you get to the leg shaping on the jumper patterns.

Some of the patterns are knitted from the top down, which means you can try them on your dog as you knit. The coats are easy to lay on your dog's back, checking them for any length adjustments that might be needed.

And don't forget that knitting is so forgiving! It stretches and relaxes, so generally the patterns will fit the breeds they are designed for. Remember, Galgos and lurchers have a similar shaped body to Greyhounds so Buster's jumper is ideal for them too.

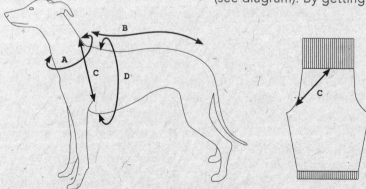

Top Tips

We all have our own ways but here are a few tips that might help you when using this book.

❖ Always have a notebook handy to mark off rows and stitch counts.

❖ When casting on, place a marker after every 10 stitches to make counting easy. If you get distracted, you will know how many stitches you have cast on.

❖ When working cables, I prefer to use a cable hook, and I always put the stitches back onto the left-hand needle to knit, rather than knitting them from the cable needle itself.

❖ My go-to cast on is the cable cast on, as it gives a well-defined edge.

❖ If the pattern is finished in rib, cast off in rib, knitting the knits and purling the purls as you cast off.

❖ Knit with good needles that feel comfortable in your hands. My favourites are vintage plastic. Use a light coloured pair for dark yarn and a dark coloured pair for light yarn to make it easier to see your stitches.

❖ Learn to 'read' your knitting, allowing you to see what you should be doing next without having to constantly refer to the pattern. For example, if you are doing a moss stitch you can start to 'read' where you need to knit and where you need to purl.

❖ If you want to get a fit that relates to the guide measurements, it is important to do a tension square. If your square comes up small, try using bigger needles, or if it is too big, try smaller needles.

❖ When knitting in the round, keep the right side of your knitting on the inside, so that you are always looking at the right side. This makes it easier to 'read' the knitting as you go.

❖ When a pattern calls for you to pick up stitches for edges or legs, have the right side facing then your first row will be a wrong side row.

❖ Feel free to use a substitute yarn from your stash but check your tension square against the one quoted in the pattern to ensure your jumper won't be teeny tiny or too baggy. Nobody wants a disappointed dog when the jumper won't fit!

❖ I often knit patterns in different yarns, but be mindful that if it calls for an Aran yarn, substitue for another Aran; I have added tips for alternative choices.

❖ Measure your dog before you start. This will tell you if you need to add extra length, or more in the chest. If your dog has a chest 2cm bigger than the pattern states and you know that you get 2 stitches to 1cm, you will need to make 2 more increases in the chest area. Make a note on the pattern before you begin.

❖ Overall, enjoy knitting your dog a jumper or blanket, no dog jumper is worth getting stressed over and remember: you can always unpick and start again, or even knit another one!